THE COUNTERWEIGHT

By: Dale D. McGinnis

I. INTRODUCTION

The recent Supreme Court decision from *Clapper*[1] has left the growing concern of secret government surveillance between a rock and a hard place. Where the debate was once shrouded by two diverging views[2], the decision has slanted towards one side leaving the other lost in the dark. This Article's goal

---

[1] Clapper v. Amnesty, 133 S. Ct. 1338, 1142 (2013).

[2] Scott Michelman, Who Can Sue Over Government Surveillance, 57 UCLA L. Rev. 71, 72 (2009).

is to provide the following: 1) a historical perspective, 2) the facts, 3) the majority's issue and holding, 4) the majority's analysis, 5) the dissent's issue and opinion, and 6) the dissent's analysis. Lastly, this article's goal is to provide an analysis and possible solution for future cases.

II.   HISTORICAL PERSPECTIVE

The United States government has a duty to protect its citizens. The Constitution of the United States separates the branches of its goverment limiting their power. Under

[3] U.S. Const. art. III, § 2.

Article III[3] of our Constitution, each branch performs checks and balances on each other. An example of this occurs where the federal courts of the judicial branch check the other branches through a process referred to as Judicial Review. However, the federal court's ability to hear certain "cases" and "controversies" is also limited by the constitution, in order to prevent the judicial process from usurping the powers of the other political branches[4]. One of the elements

---

[4] Id. supra note 2 at 1146, 1147.

limiting this process within the Amendment is standing[5].

Throughout history conflicts with foreign powers and the threat of terrorist attacks such as the Red Scare, the Cold War, and 9/11[6], force our government to balance our Constitutional rights with its duty to protect its citizens. In order to balance and check this power of the Executive branch, the Foreign Intelligence Surveillance Act (FISC) was enacted in 1978[7], amended to broaden its

---

[5] Id. supra note 2 at 1146.

[6] Id. supra note 3 at 74.

[7] Id. supra note 3 at 72.

power in 2008[8] following 9/11 after a Foreign

Intelligence Surveillance Court Judge

narrowed its authorization of foreign

surveillance[9], and may need to undergo

Judicial Review. But, standing requires that

the plaintiff show the following: 1) an injury-

in-fact, 2) a causal connection between this

injury and the statute, and 3) that the decision

is likely to redress the injury[10]. Because any

relaxation of the standing requirement is

directly related to the expansion of judicial

---

[8] Id. supra note 3 at 73.

[9] Id. supra note 3 at 74.

[10] Id. supra note 2 at 1147, 1148.

power[11], the courts are naturally hesitant in order to maintain balance.

In 1972, *Laird v. Tatum* [12]was heard. The court addressed secret government surveillance for the first time. In a 5-4 divide, the court stated: 1) an injury-in-fact may be present and ongoing or based on prospective government action; it must fall under the scope of the implicate statue, and affect the plaintiff in an individual way; future injuries based on the prospective government action are only injuries-in-fact when they reach a

---

[11] Id. supra note 2 at 1146, 1147.

[12] Id. supra note 3 at 74.

certain likelihood; and, the plaintiff cannot assert a future injury based on a subjective fear that he will be affect by the government action[13]. 2) The plaintiff must show a causal nexus exist between his injury and the conduct being challenged, he can assert this right even if he is not the target of a defendant's action or when his injury is not a direct product of the defendant's action[14]; and 3) the judicial remedy sought must directly correct the plaintiff's injury[15].

---

[13] Id. supra note 3 at 74, 75.

[14] Id. supra note 3 at 75, 76.

[15] Id.

However after cases proceeding *Laird,* several courts addressed specifically required for an injury-in-fact. The broad approach required only a reasonable likelihood-not a certainty-of ongoing or future injury[16], and the restrained approach required the injury be "concrete and particularized" harm that is "actual" or "imminent rather than "conjectural" or "hypothetical"[17]. A loss of one's privacy has been well established as an injury sufficient to confer standing[18].

---

[16] Id. supra note 3 at 90.

[17] Id. supra note 2 at 5, 6.

[18] Id. supra note 3 at 79.

However, it is difficult to establish that one, is in-fact, being spied[19] on because the government conducts these programs in secret and often invokes, the state secrets privilege baring parties and courts from obtaining any information if there is a reasonable danger that the disclosure will expose military matters, which in the interest of national security should not be divulged[20]. Therefore, because of the difficulty of proving standing based a present injury, it is easier for the plaintiff to prove a "chilling

[19] Id.

[20] Id. supra note 3 at 80.

effect" because the evidence lies with the plaintiffs, which is the affect of the surveillance programs restricting or preventing protected freedoms such as speech and association[21]. Up until *Clapper*, the Supreme Court of the United States had not addressed or commented on the threshold for a "chilling effect": whether it was a reasonable likelihood of injury, a certainty or imminent injury, or somewhere in between in the context of secret government surveillance.[22]

---

[21] Id. supra note 3 at 81.

[22] Elisa Sielski, Clapper v. Amnesty Interntional: Who Has Standing to Challenge Government Surveillance?, 8 Duke J. Const.

III.   FACTS

Attorneys and human rights, labor, legal and media organizations, which as United States citizens, filed a claim against the government declaring FISA's Act § 1881a unconstitutional, and requested an injunction against the surveillance authorized by the provision[23]. The attorneys represented clients who have been acquitted of terrorism charges, faced criminal charges proceeding 9/11, are detainees at Guantanamo Bay, Cuba, and communicate by telephone and email with

Law & PP Sidebar 51, 54 (2013).

[23] Id. supra note 2 at 1145.

people outside the United States such as: experts, investigators, attorneys, family member, and others who are located abroad that prior to 2008 were the target of government surveillance[24]. The human rights researchers conduct work where they track down people claimed to be associated with terrorist organizations by the CIA in other countries where they are tortured, involving communication by telephone and email with former detainees, layers for detainees, relatives of detainees, political activists,

---

[24] Id. supra note 2 at 1157.

journalists, and fixers all over the world[25].

The United States District Court for Southern

New York found the respondents had lacked

standing, but the United States Court of

Appeals for the Second Circuit reversed

stating: because there is an objectively

reasonable likelihood that their

communications would be intercepted at

some time in the future, the respondents have

undergone costly and burdensome measures,

such as flying to these countries to speak

directly with their clients, to protect the

---

[25] Id. supra note 2 at 1156, 1157.

confidentiality of their international

communications from possible §1881a

surveillance[26].

IV.   ISSUE AND HOLDING OF THE

COURT

An injury must be "certainly impending"

to constitute an injury in fact[27]. The

respondents asserted they suffered injury in

fact that is fairly to § 1881a because of there

is an objectively reasonable likelihood that

their communications with their foreign

contacts will be intercepted under § 1881a at

[26] Id. supra note 2 at 1157.

[27] Id. supra note 2 at 1147, 1148.

some point, and the court held 1) that this standard is inconsistent with the threatened injury requirement by the Court, 2) the claims rest on a speculative chain of possibilities that does not establish their potential injury is certainly impending, 3) their costs are the product of this speculative fear of surveillance, and 4) the result of this case does not insulate § 1881a from judicial review[28].

V.   ANALYSIS OF THE COURT

---

[28] Id. supra note 2 at 1148,1149,1150.

The "objectively reasonable likelihood" standard is inconsistent with the requirement that the "threatened injury must be certainly impending to constitute injury in fact."[29] The Court places the respondent's argument in the real of highly speculative fear of: 1) targeting by the government for surveillance, 2) choice of the government to invoke § 188a, 3) the FISC Judge will authorize the Government's request, 4) the government will succeed in intercepting the communication of the respondents' contacts, and 5) the respondents

---

[29] Id.

will be parties to the particular communications the government intercepts[30].

Because the respondents have no knowledge of the United State's targeting practices, even if they target their contract; use the FISC and § 1881a; they obtain approval from FISC; only speculation exists whether the government would be successful in acquiring their contacts communications and whether their own communications would be with those contacts[31]. Therefore, because they do not face a threat of "certainly

[30] Id.

[31] Id.

17

impending" interception under § 1881a, the respondent's injury are merely the product of this fear of surveillance, and is insufficient to create standing[32].

Furthermore, the holding of this case in no one insulates § 1881a from judicial review[33]. The FISC evaluates the government's certifications, targeting procedures, and minimization procedures, which comport with the Fourth Amendment[34]. If the government intended to disclose any

---

[32] Id.

[33] Id.

[34] Id.

information obtained from § 1881a or

prosecute one of the respondent-attorney's

foreign clients, they must provide advance

notice of its intent, and the affected person

may challenge the lawfulness of the

acquisition[35].

VI.   ISSUE AND OPINION OF THE

DISSENT

The basic question is whether the injury,

the interception is "actual or imminent"[36].

Based upon the record along with

commonsense inferences, there is a very high

[35] Id.

[36] Id.

likelihood that government, acting under the authority of § 1881a, will intercept at least some of the communications[37]. Furthermore, federal courts frequently entertain actions for injunctions and for declaratory relief aimed at preventing future activities that are reasonably likely or highly likely, but not absolutely certain to take place, which is all that is needed to support standing[38].

VII.   ANALYSIS OF THE DISSENT

Plaintiffs have engaged, and will continue to engage, in electronic

[37] Id.

[38] Id.

communications of a kind that the 2008

amendment, but not the prior Act, authorizes

the government to intercept, which include:

discussions with family members of those

detained at Guantanamo, friends and

acquaintances of those persons, and

investigators', experts, and others with

knowledge of circumstances related to

terrorist activities[39]. These persons are located

outside the United States, they are not foreign

powers or agents, and they exchange foreign

intelligence information that relates to

---

[39] Id. supra note 2 at 1158, 1159.

international terrorism and the national

defense or the security of the United States[40].

Plaintiffs have a strong motive to engage

in, and the government has a strong motive to

listen to, conversations of the kind which:

concern suspected foreign terrorist, involve

their families, colleagues, and contacts, and

concern what they have done or said, relating

to terrorist activities, concern the political,

social and commercial environments in which

the suspected terrorist have lived and worked[41].

The government seeks to learn as much as

[40] Id.

[41] Id.

they reasonably can learn about suspected terrorist, as well as their contacts and activities, along with those of friends and family members, and they are motived by a desire to convict those whom they believe are guilty; but also, by the critical and overriding need to protect America from terrorism[42].

The government has the capacity to conduct electrometric surveillance on the plaintiffs because of the technology available, rarely files requests that fail to meet the statutory criteria (In 2011, of the 1,676

---

[42] Id. supra note 2 at 1159.

applications, two were withdrawn, and 30 were modified[43]), and § 1881a simplifies and thus expedites the approval process, making it more likely that the government will use it to obtain the necessary approval.[44] Based on 1) similarity of content, 2) strong motives, 3) prior behavior, and 4) capacity; inferences point to a very strong likelihood that the government will intercept at least some of the plaintiffs' communications, and no special factors exists to suggest otherwise[45].

---

[43] Id.

[44] Id.

[45] Id. supra note 2 at 1160.

Imminence is an elastic concept, and the Court's holding in other standing cases show that standing exists here: 1) Realistic and impending threat, not a certainty, that the candidate's opponent would do so at the time the plaintiff filed the complaint, 2) a genuine threat of enforcement was likely sufficient, and 3) due to generalized concern about exposure to radiation and the apprehension flowing from the uncertainty about the health and genetic consequence of even small emissions[46].

---

[46] Id.

A. AUTHOR'S ANALYSIS

The future is inherently uncertain[47].
With plaintiffs suffering injuries that become
next to impossible to prove, proving future
injuries or "chilling effects" became the
pinnacle of debate in and outside the context
of secret government surveillance. Before
Clapper, the debate over *Larid* split between
a broad and restrained interpretation of
standing in the context of secret government
surveillance: whether an objective reasonable
likelihood or certainly imminent injury would

---

[47] Id.

suffice. Imminence is known as an elastic concept therefore *Clapper* was hoped to become a beacon of light amidst the fog blurring the line between the broad and restrained view.

1) Reasonable Likelihood and Certainly Imminent

In the context of secret government Surveillance, *Larid* became the transcription, which lower courts used in their interpretation of standing[48]. One District Court only allowed standing when the

---

[48] Id. supra note 3 at 90.

chilling effect is the result of "regulatory, proscriptive, or compulsory" government action, which did not encompass government surveillance[49]. The other view, backed up by two Supreme Court opinions and several federal appellate decisions, bared claims of chilling effects only when they were unreasonable and subjective[50]. Therefore, these two views set the stage, and the cases that followed: *Halkin* (subjective chilling)[51], *United Presbyterian* (order involved no

---

[49] Id.

[50] Id.

[51] Id. supra note 3 at 91.

commands, no prohibitions to these plaintiffs, and set forth no standard governing their conduct)[52], *ACLU v. NSA* (injury deriving solely from the fear of secret government surveillance)[53], and *Socialist Workers Party v. Attorney General* (holding standing because the allegations were much more specific and would have concrete effects of dissuading activity and rejecting the "regulatory, proscriptive, or compulsory" requirement)[54], *Presbyterian Church v.*

---

[52] Id.

[53] Id. supra note 3 at 92.

[54] Id. supra note 3 at 99.

United States (a concrete demonstrable decrease in attendance producing an objective chill effect)[55], and *Muslin Community Association of Ann Arbor v. Ashcroft* (producing a chilling effect from a Section 215 order to produce books, papers, and records).[56]

Outside the context of secret government surveillance but in accordance with chilling effects, *Ozonoff v. Berzak* (rights being chilled by mere existence, without more, the physical effect was speculative but the

[55] Id. supra note 3 at 94.

[56] Id. supra note 3 at 95.

chilling effect it produced was not)[57], *Clark v. Library of Congress* (producing an objective chill standing based on the effects the investigation had on Clark's beliefs and associations)[58], and *Meese* (high likelihood of illegal campaign funding)[59]. However, whether inside or outside the context of secret government surveillance, though the broad and restrained view of a "chilling effect" set the stage in the eye of the storm; from outside, a larger debate raged.

---

[57] Id.

[58] Id.

[59] Id. supra note 3 at 96.

2) Balances: National Security and a

Future Injury; Expansion of

Judicial Review and Separation of

Powers

From the perspective of the Supreme

Court Justice's, the debate over "chilling

effect" was not primarily a topic of actual,

imminent, or reasonable likelihood of an

injury, but a balance with National Security.

On one hand, since 9/11 and other

scares, the Court's had to consider whether

their decisions would hinder the

government's duty to protect its citizens by

monitoring, intercepting, and collecting any electronic information, which could take the form of emails or telephone calls. Although standing refers to the Judicial Branch's power to hear certain "cases" and "controversies", the expansion of this power through Judicial Review could create an imbalance between the separation of powers, and more specifically, affect this ability given to the government by the Executive Branch.

Vice Versa, standing addresses injuries by plaintiffs as a result of injury-in-fact. If the Justice's or Court's ignored these injuries as fears produced as byproducts of speculation, then a limitation of their power through Judicial Review could create an imbalances between the separation of powers aggregating the amendments of the constitution. Therefore, in *Clapper*, the courts have and will continue to sidebar the entire debate, until a "case" or "controversy" can find be identified which will be used to push the scales, on either side. This "case" or "controversy" requires counterweight.

B. A Possible Solution: The Counterweight

A counterweight is a weight which, when used properly, is used to prevent an unfair tipping of the scales. In theory, a certain "case" or "controversy" could be used as a counterweight to balance: National Security and a future Injury with the expansion of Judicial Review and the Separation of Powers. In order for this theory to work, the parts must be identifiable: 1) the frame, 2) the beam, and lastly 3) the counterweight.

1) The Frame

The frame is the most easily identifiable part. It is simply the Constitution of the United States of America amendments[60]. These amendments setup the foundation and structure for the theory, which limit and provide movement and weight for each of the following parts.

2) The Beam

The beam is merely a part of the frame. Like the frame, the beam is a part of the Constitution. Specifically, it would include the Third Amendment of the Constitution,

---

[60] Id. supre note 4.

which limits each side of the device

determining their weight and/or power

(Separation of Powers).

3) The Counterweight

The counterweight would be a force,

idea, or influence that counteracts or

compensates each side producing the desired

balancing effect. So far, various cases have

been addressed on the plaintiff's side

concerning but not limited the following

injuries: environmental, endangered species,

loss of privacy, behavior changes in religious,

filing job applications, and social activities,

campaign funding, and loss of money in order to secure privacy of clients[61]. The government, on the other hand, has suffered very little damage. However, they have retained the ability to protect its citizens' National Security.

Therefore, considering the government has suffered no injury but has compensated the plaintiff's with this sort of protection in the context of secret government surveillance, the "case" or "controversy" would need a plaintiff, force, idea, or influence with a

---

[61] Id. supra note 23 at 60.

factor that would compensate the government, which would counteract the worries of the Court over the expansion of Judicial Review and Separation of Powers with the concerns over National Security and the inherent uncertainty of a future injury. This plaintiff, force, idea, or influence would need to counterbalance the uncertainty of a future injury and the growing scare of National Security with the need for Expansion of Judicial Review and the effect it would have on the Separation of Powers. This could take the form of legislation as well.

With the right influence, a bill or amendment could be passed to counteract the insolvencies present.

C. CONCLUSION

With the debate over secret government surveillance between National Security and an inherently uncertain future injury and over the expansion of Judicial Review and the Separation of Powers, the recent decision from *Clapper* has left a standing shroud of mystery. However, a plaintiff, force, idea, or influence could counterbalance the subtle differences, and clarify the standing required by the Courts and possibly compensate the Plaintiffs for future injury involving secret government surveillance. Though the nature of the counterweight remains a mystery, it may provide a beacon of light amidst the blurred line between the broad and restrain view for future cases.

www.ingramcontent.com/pod-product-compliance
Lightning Source LLC
Chambersburg PA
CBHW030738180526
45157CB00008BA/3223